ICE HOCKEY LEGENDS

Martin Brodeur

Sergei Fedorov

Peter Forsberg

Wayne Gretzky

Dominik Hasek

Brett Hull

Jaromir Jagr

Paul Kariya

John LeClair

Mario Lemieux

Eric Lindros

Mark Messier

CHELSEA HOUSE PUBLISHERS

ICE HOCKEY LEGENDS

SERGEI FEDOROV

Dean Schabner

CHELSEA HOUSE PUBLISHERS

Philadelphia

Produced by P. M. Gordon Associates
Philadelphia, Pennsylvania

Picture research by Gillian Speeth, Picture This

CHELSEA HOUSE PUBLISHERS

Editor in Chief: Stephen Reginald
Managing Editor: James Gallagher
Production Manager: Pamela Loos
Art Director: Sara Davis
Director of Photography: Judy L. Hasday
Senior Production Editor: Lisa Chippendale
Publishing Coordinator: James McAvoy
Project Editor: Becky Durost Fish
Cover Design and Digital Illustration: Keith Trego

Cover Photos: AP/Wide World Photos

The Chelsea House World Wide Web site address is
http://www.chelseahouse.com

First Printing

1 3 5 7 9 8 6 4 2

Library of Congress Cataloging-in-Publication Data

Schabner, Dean.
    Sergei Fedorov / Dean Schabner.
       p. cm. — (Ice hockey legends)
    Includes bibliographical references (p.) and index.
    Summary: A biography of Sergei Fedorov, the Russian
hockey star who helped the Detroit Red Wings win the stanley Cup in 1997 and 1998.
    ISBN 0-7910-5012-2
    1. Fedorov, Sergei, 1969– —Juvenile literature.
2. Hockey players—Russia (Federation)—Biography—Juvenile
literature. 3. Detroit Red Wings (Hockey team)—Juvenile literature. [1. Fedorov, Sergei, 1969– . 2. Hockey players.]
I. Title. II. Series.
GV848.5.F43S32 1998
796.962'092—dc21   98-31351
[B]   CIP
                                                              AC

CONTENTS

CHAPTER 1
A POWER PLAY 7

CHAPTER 2
FLIGHT TO THE WINGS 13

CHAPTER 3
ARRIVAL AND ADJUSTMENT 23

CHAPTER 4
TRIUMPH AND DISAPPOINTMENT 31

CHAPTER 5
A BROKEN WING? 37

CHAPTER 6
BACK IN THE GAME 51

STATISTICS 58
CHRONOLOGY 59
FURTHER READING 61
INDEX 63

One night in February 1998, Sergei Fedorov faced two sets of opponents as he skated onto the ice at Joe Louis Arena in Detroit. This was his first appearance for the Detroit Red Wings since the previous June, when the team had won the Stanley Cup, the National Hockey League's championship trophy.

One set of opponents was the visiting team on the ice, the Florida Panthers. The other group was in the stands—the fans who thought Fedorov had put money ahead of team loyalty.

Fedorov is considered to be among the greatest players in hockey. A high-scoring forward with blinding speed, he is not afraid to battle the bruising defensemen against the boards for the puck. And once he has the puck on his stick, he loves to pass it to a teammate at just the right moment. His love of setting up his teammates is so great that sometimes, after beating a goalie himself, he

Sergei Fedorov skates during practice on February 27, 1998—the day of his return to the Detroit Red Wings after a salary dispute.

will drop the puck off to allow someone else to score the goal. His coaches and teammates have often told him to be more selfish.

By September 1997 he had been a Red Wing for seven years, since defecting from Russia to join the National Hockey League (NHL). But when the rest of the Red Wings went back to work after a summer of basking in the glow of their championship, Fedorov did not join them. The Red Wings' owners had said they were not ready to pay him what he felt he deserved, and Fedorov decided to hold out. Before training camp began, he asked the team to trade him. The front office refused. So when camp opened in September, the young Russian stayed home.

For the next seven months, the game was played in the media. Fedorov said he wanted only what was fair, and at first Detroit fans took his side. Stories that he was keeping in shape by training with the Russian Central Red Army team in Moscow raised fans' sympathy for him. But when other reports said he was spending his time on the beaches in Florida, Italy, and the Bahamas, or following his friend Anna Kournikova on the professional tennis tour, public opinion shifted. Even his teammates started to say that Sergei had become selfish, that he cared only about money.

The troubles with his teammates had actually begun before the contract problem. A few days after the Red Wings won the Stanley Cup in June 1997, a limousine carrying two of the players crashed. Everyone in the car was injured, but the person hurt the most was Russian Vladimir Konstantinov—Fedorov's best friend on the team. "For me, the party was over when the accident happened," Fedorov later explained. "Right after that, the next day, I didn't feel like I won the Cup. I didn't want to celebrate, and I still don't."

When Fedorov's three other Russian teammates took the Stanley Cup on a celebratory visit to Russia, Fedorov decided not to go. Defenseman Slava Fetisov and forward Igor Larionov interpreted this as an insult to them and to their homeland. And when Fedorov began his holdout, they said they didn't care if he ever came back.

In January 1998, when Russia was drawing up its team for the winter Olympics in Nagano, Japan, Fedorov's name was left off the list, even though players with much less skill were included. At the last minute, when a forward went down with an injury, Fedorov was added to the team.

In Japan it soon became clear that if Fedorov had spent the last few months on a beach, there must have been a hockey rink nearby. Through the first four games of Russia's march to the silver medal, Fedorov led his team in minutes played and in total points (goals plus assists). He seemed to have lost none of his speed or toughness and none of his love for the game.

The NHL took notice. During the Olympic Games, the Carolina Hurricanes offered him a six-year, $38-million contract. Fedorov accepted, but

Fedorov watches his friend Anna Kournikova play tennis at the U.S. Open in August 1997. During his holdout from the Red Wings, Detroit fans were upset by news reports that he spent most of his time following the tennis tour.

by league rules, Detroit had the right to match the deal and keep him. At the last minute, though Fedorov had declared he would not play for Detroit again, the Red Wings did match the offer.

The next day, Fedorov took the ice at Joe Louis Arena with the teammates he had abandoned six months earlier. Red Wings owner Mike Ilitch, the man who in 1990 had helped Fedorov leave Russia for the NHL, came to the locker room to greet the returning star. The two men shook hands and agreed that their conflict had been merely business. Fedorov promised he'd earn every penny that he was being paid.

Making peace with the fans would not be so

Winning back the fans: after his first practice with the team following his holdout, Fedorov signs autographs.

easy. When Fedorov came out for warmups, there were more boos than cheers from the stands. He knew he'd have to win the fans back slowly—by playing hockey as well as he possibly could.

That night, none of Fedorov's breakneck rushes from one end of the ice to the other resulted in a goal, but his teammates and the fans caught glimpses of the player they had waited 51 games for. He showed the same sense he'd always had for getting the puck to the right man. His pass ahead to Nicklas Lidstrom led to the first goal of the night. Even Igor Larionov, one of the harshest critics during Fedorov's holdout, admitted that Sergei had made a few plays that night that only he could have made.

After the game, Fedorov said he felt like a balloon, light-headed from the excitement of playing again. He had helped his teammates defeat the opponents on the ice. The other opponents, the ones in the stands, he had just begun to win back.

FLIGHT TO THE WINGS

In July 1990 Russia was still part of the Soviet Union, the communist-controlled superpower that was on the verge of breaking up. But while politics in the Soviet Union descended into turmoil, the Soviet hockey team was in Portland, Oregon, preparing for the Goodwill Games.

Sergei Fedorov, one of the Soviet players, stood up after a team meal, said he had forgotten his hotel room key, and left the restaurant. Instead of going back to his room, though, Fedorov went outside to meet representatives of the Detroit Red Wings, who took him to team owner Mike Ilitch's private jet and flew him to Detroit.

Two days later, while the Soviets fumed, Ilitch announced that Fedorov had signed a five-year deal with the Red Wings. The young star did not attend the news conference—not because he was embarrassed about his inability to speak English, but for a much bigger reason: the Red Wings, the

During the Soviet team's 1990 tour of North America, the 20-year-old Fedorov looks toward his future.

NHL, and the Soviet authorities had been sling-
ing accusations at one another since Fedorov dis-
appeared, and he wanted no part of that.

His decision to leave Russia was not political.
As he explained later, he just wanted to play hockey, a lot of hockey, with the best players in the
world. And from what he had seen when the Central Red Army team played an exhibition series
against NHL teams in the winter of 1989–90, the
NHL had the best players in the world. He also
liked the idea of an 80-game season, rather than
the approximately 40 games played in the Soviet
leagues. He liked playing two or three times a
week. Perhaps most surprisingly, he liked the
banging, the pounding, the physical style found
on the small rinks of the NHL.

But Fedorov still thought of himself as Russian.
He loved his homeland, where he had left friends
and family. He wanted to be able to return, and
he didn't want people thinking badly of him or his
family. If he had appeared at the news conference,
Russians might have taken his defection as an
insult. So he stayed away, and his only comment
came through a team official who said Fedorov
wanted everyone to know that he had always been
happy playing for the Soviet national teams and
that he hoped to play for his homeland in the
future.

Fedorov did not apply for political asylum in the
United States. He just asked that his visitor's visa
be changed to a temporary work visa. He did not
say much of anything until the furor died down.
And then at last he made his position clear: he
had come to America for the hockey.

Russians had not begun playing ice hockey until
the 1940s. Before that, they played a game called
bandy, which takes place on an area of ice the

size of a soccer field. It features 11 people on a side, with sticks resembling those used in field hockey.

The first recorded exhibition of North American hockey in Russia was held in February 1946 in Moscow. Following a bandy match, some of the players set up crude boards to enclose an area roughly the size of a Canadian hockey rink. There they displayed the game they had learned from their World War II allies. The fans liked it, and when the soccer season ended the following fall, a hockey league was created.

It would be another 10 years before the first indoor rinks were built in the Soviet Union. Until then, games were played on frozen rivers or ponds, with fans gathered around the boards, cheering enthusiastically to keep warm.

This lack of rinks might seem a disadvantage, but it led to the training system that helped the Soviets become the preeminent power in international hockey for four decades. Their so-called land training—which featured a regimen of cycling, running, weight training, and calisthenics that only recently has become standard for NHL players—helped create powerful, tireless athletes.

Moreover, because they did not play on rinks with reliable boards, Russians did not learn the "dump and chase" style of hockey, in which a defenseman will clear the puck hard out of his zone, knowing that it will bounce back off the boards for a forward to pick up. Instead, the Russians learned a puck-control game, using deft stickhandling and precision passes to move the puck up the ice.

The legacy of bandy and soccer also inspired another difference in the Russian game. While players in North American hockey traditionally kept to one area of the ice—left wings on the left, right wings on the right, centers up the center—Russians grew up playing a more fluid, circling game.

Whatever can be said for their style, the Russian mastery of hockey was so quick and so complete that in the 10 Olympic Games between 1956 and 1992, the Soviets failed to win the gold medal in the sport only twice.

This was the tradition in which Fedorov grew up. He was born in 1969 in Pskov, a city of less than 500,000 people in western Russia, near the borders of Latvia and Estonia. When he was nine, his father—a hockey coach—moved the family to the town of Apatiti, above the Arctic Circle near Finland.

In a country with few indoor rinks, the long winters were a blessing to the young hockey player. He played every day when the river was frozen. On weekends and when it was too cold to go to school, he would stay on the ice for six or seven hours, taking breaks only to sip hot tea from a samovar that was kept lit on the bank.

Fedorov says he owes not only his skills but also his vision of the game to his father, Viktor Alexandrovich Fedorov. When people marvel at his speed, Fedorov remembers his father's teaching—the first five steps are the most important. When they wonder at his agility and his ability to make precision turns, he remembers that he and his friends would practice skating around a plant that had grown up through the ice, watching the top of the stem as they turned. He still recalls exactly how that plant looked, frozen in the gray ice. Though his formal education ended with high school, Fedorov comes across as a thoughtful man, and he credits his father for that as well.

Before he was 13, his hockey playing had drawn the attention of the sports machine of the Soviet Union, and by the time he was 16 he was playing for the Central Red Army team. The Soviet authorities sought out the most talented young athletes in the country and made sure that they received the best training in the finest facilities in the land. The success of Soviet athletes in international competition, and in the Olympics in particular, was a point of great national pride.

Fedorov was invited to move from his quiet provincial town in the frozen north to Moscow, where he could receive the full attention of the best Soviet teachers and coaches. He accepted, and in Moscow he got the chance to play with other budding talents, including future NHL stars Pavel Bure and Aleksandr Mogilny. But he also had to deal with being away from his family and friends.

He was in awe at first, finding himself training alongside his idol, the great forward Sergei Makarov, and the other giants of Soviet hockey in

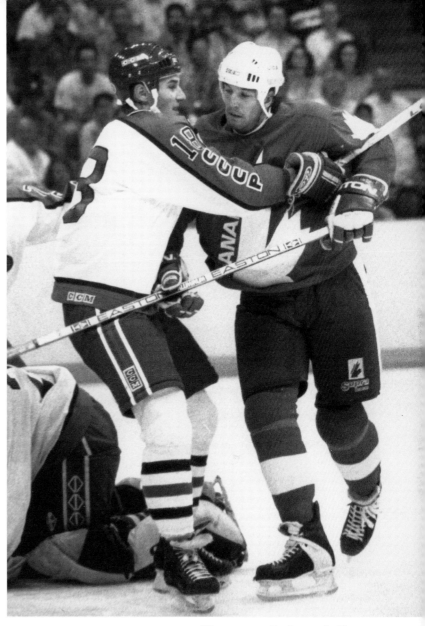

The young Fedorov (left) caught the NHL's attention when he played for Soviet teams in international tournaments. Here he tangles with future teammate Brendan Shanahan.

the 1980s—Igor Larionov, Aleksei Kasatonov, and Slava Fetisov—under the guidance of the architect of the Soviet Union's hockey dominance, Viktor Tikhonov. Although stardom was reserved for players who had established their greatness year after year, young players like Fedorov, Bure, Alexei Yashin, and Mogilny got recognition for the potential they showed. When others might be turned away from a crowded restaurant, Fedorov and his friends would be let in. It embarrassed him, he said, to receive special treatment, but it felt nice, too. He knew that the great hockey players he idolized all received that kind of treatment, and he wanted to be like them, on and off the ice.

From 1985 through 1990 he played for the Central Red Army team. He first drew international attention in 1988, playing on the silver-medal-winning Soviet squad at the World Junior Championships. In just six games he scored six goals and was credited with six assists. Then in 1989 and again in 1990, he led the Soviet team to gold medals at the World Championships. During the winter of 1989–90, the Central Red Army team toured the NHL.

It was during those tournaments—face-to-face with the best North Americans—that Fedorov started thinking about the NHL. And while Fedorov was eyeing the NHL, the NHL was looking him over, too. Red Wings captain Steve Yzerman, after playing head-to-head with Fedorov in the 1989 World Championships in Stockholm, Sweden, was so impressed that he mentioned the youngster to the team's management. Soon the Red Wings decided to select Fedorov in the 1989 NHL draft.

Yzerman and Fedorov met again in April 1990 during a tournament in Bern, Switzerland. This time they talked a little bit, and Fedorov was pleased by the attention of an NHL player whose style resembled his own—a quick, powerful skater who excelled at both offense and defense.

Not everyone, though, was ready to welcome the Soviets and other Eastern Europeans to the NHL with open arms. Despite the Soviet dominance of Olympic hockey, many thought the Russians would not do well in the rough-and-tumble NHL. In the late 1980s, when the Soviet Hockey Federation finally allowed a few of its aging stars to join the NHL (in exchange for a fee payable to the homeland), the Russians did not make a strong impression. Players like Igor Larionov and Sergei Priakin were wonderfully skilled and tougher than some people had expected, but still they struggled to adjust. The physical style played on the smaller rinks of North America was difficult for men who had made their careers in the wide-open international game. And the Soviets were not interested in letting their younger players join the National Hockey League, where—under the rules that prevailed at the time—they would become ineligible for the Olympics.

The first real glimpse of what was to come occurred in the 1989–90 season. Mogilny had defected to join the NHL after the 1989 World Championships in Anchorage, Alaska. Mogilny had a couple of the flaws that NHL experts considered typical of Eastern Europeans: he was susceptible to being bumped, banged, and muscled, and he was moody. But most of the time he seemed faster than anybody else on the ice, and what he could do with the puck, even as a 20-year-old rookie, looked like magic.

As the NHL watched Mogilny with fascination and amazement that year, another fan was keeping a close watch on his career—from halfway

Aleksandr (Alexander) Mogilny in 1989, shortly after he defected from the Soviet Union to join the Buffalo Sabres.

around the world. Sergei Fedorov, who had been Mogilny's roommate before his defection, was eager to see how his former linemate fared in the National Hockey League.

In the weeks leading up to Mogilny's jump to the NHL, the two young men had not talked about a possible future in North America, even though Mogilny had already been drafted by the Buffalo Sabres. But Fedorov could not miss the signs that Mogilny was looking for an opportunity to leave the Soviet team. During a stop in Stockholm, Sweden, Mogilny walked out of the team's hotel and did not come back. "By the end I knew he was going," Fedorov later said. "I didn't know the details, but I knew. I came back to the room to say good-bye. He asked me if I wanted to come. But [in early 1989] I hadn't been drafted. I had nowhere to go. I told him, 'What am I going to defect to?'"

Mogilny's rookie season convinced NHL teams that the young Russians had plenty to offer. The Red Wings, who had gambled by selecting Fedorov with a fourth-round pick in the 1989 draft, tried unsuccessfully to convince the Soviets to release him. By the time the Russian team came to the United States for the Goodwill Games in the summer of 1990, the Russian authorities must have known something was coming. Yet their security measures were not sufficient to keep Fedorov from walking away from the team dinner on July 22, before the Goodwill Games even began.

ARRIVAL AND ADJUSTMENT

The announcement that, for the second time in a year, one of the greatest young hockey players of the Soviet Union had abandoned his homeland for the riches of the NHL caused shock waves around the world. The Soviet Hockey Federation thought it had worked out a deal with the NHL. The two sides had hammered out a pact that said, at least in the minds of the Soviets, that NHL teams would not help players defect. The NHL would accept the over-the-hill players the Soviets were ready to provide, paying the Soviets needed cash in return.

When Soviet hockey authorities claimed that the Red Wings had violated the deal, NHL officials told them that if they could produce a valid contract showing that Fedorov was obligated to play for a Soviet team, the young star would be denied permission to play in the NHL. No such contract was produced. The Soviets made further demands,

On his way to leading all NHL rookies in scoring, Fedorov handles the puck against the Anaheim Mighty Ducks.

On the first day on the ice at his first NHL training camp in September 1990, Fedorov (right) looks to teammates Shawn Burr (left) and Daniel Shank for guidance. Later he said he felt like a dog during his early days in North America because he understood only simple words.

even threatening to boycott a 29-game exhibition series between Soviet and North American teams. In the end, the Red Wings agreed to pay a signing fee to the Soviets, and the furor died down.

Aside from all the controversy he brought to the NHL, Fedorov came into the league with a different reputation from that of most other Eastern European players. He had the speed, stickhandling, and flashy moves for which the Russians have always been known, but added to that was an almost Canadian attraction to the physical side of the game. A good hard thump wouldn't send

Fedorov into a cocoon—in fact, it seemed to inspire him.

But the Red Wings knew Fedorov would have adjustment difficulties both on and off the ice. In 1985, when Czechoslovakia's Petr Klima defected to play for Detroit, the team had learned how difficult it can be for a player to fit into a new and different culture. The Red Wings set Fedorov up with a house and a car, and they immediately enrolled him in intensive English classes. They made the most talkative player on the team his roommate for road trips. Fedorov says that at first he felt like a dog, understanding only single words or simple commands. But everyone from team owner Mike Ilitch to the man who filled the water bottles was prepared to make things as easy as possible for him.

Of course there were problems anyway. Early in his rookie season, Fedorov made a startling confession to his teammates. For days he told everyone on the team, "I need love." Some of his teammates turned away in embarrassment; others pretended they hadn't heard. It wasn't until Fedorov pulled out his Russian-English dictionary and pointed that he finally received the new pair of *gloves* that he needed.

In his NHL debut at New Jersey on October 4, 1990, Fedorov scored his first career power-play goal. Six days later he racked up his first two assists. Neither method of scoring would be a rare occurrence as the season went on. Fedorov led all rookies with 31 goals and 48 assists for 79 points. He was named to the All-Rookie Team and finished second to goaltending phenom Ed Belfour in voting for the Calder Trophy, the award for the league's Rookie of the Year.

Fedorov's prodigious scoring was all the more

impressive because he played on a team loaded with high-scoring centers. In fact, he was often used on defensive lines because of his combination of checking and skating skills. But for all their scoring, the Red Wings finished with a losing record, 34–38–8, third in the Norris Division. The team made the playoffs but was eliminated in the first round by St. Louis. In the seven-game play-off series, Fedorov had a goal and five assists.

Although the year was a disappointment for Red Wings fans, for Fedorov the future was bright. The young man had embraced American pop culture, taking an immediate liking to rock bands like Guns N' Roses. And Americans—at least in Detroit—took an immediate liking to him. This was no dour, gray, grim-faced Soviet. His style off the ice matched his play. He was quick to learn English, quick to smile, and eager to please the fans.

In his second NHL season, 1991–92, Fedorov may have been slowed as much by the quality of his teammates as he was by opponents. Detroit coach Bryan Murray had to find ice time for Steve Yzerman, Kelly Miller, and Jimmy Carson, all of whom played center and all of whom were proven scorers. So even though Fedorov had been the second highest scorer on the team in his rookie year, in his sophomore season Murray often used the young Russian on defensive lines. Even when he played offense, Fedorov bounced from one position to another, from center to left and right wing.

Most of the great players in any sport make their mark by playing one position, becoming specialists in a role that they perform better than anyone else. For such a player, the constant position changes that Fedorov faced could have seemed like an insult. But he flourished. As a winger he made full use of his speed on breakaways and his strength going into the corners to chase down loose pucks. On defense, Fedorov's fearless checking, his sleight of hand with his stick, his quick feet, and his ability to read what other players were going to do made him invaluable.

The pounding Fedorov had taken as a rookie, when opponents still believed that they could knock him off his game with a few hard hits, had only made him realize how much he enjoyed the physical side of the NHL game. Now, playing on the Red Wings' defensive line, Fedorov got a chance to hit back. And playing defense allowed him to showcase his most breathtaking talent—taking the puck himself from the defensive zone across center ice, skating around and through defenders, spinning, changing speeds, faking and cutting, until he faced a goaltender who was already dizzy from trying to follow the puck.

Meanwhile Fedorov continued to embrace American culture. He had learned English quickly, and he understood the way fans felt about him, comparing it with the way he felt about his favorite rock stars. When he got an autograph from a famous singer or guitar player, it made him happy. He realized that he could make his fans happy in the same way, so he often took time to sign programs or photographs—with a smile.

The Red Wings' defense improved enough in 1991–92 for Detroit to finish first in the Norris Division with a record of 43–25–12—the third best in the NHL. Still, however, this did not translate into playoff success. After a tough seven-game victory over Minnesota in the first round, the Wings were swept in four games by the Chicago Blackhawks.

That year Fedorov slightly improved his totals in both goals and assists, finishing with 86 points

In his third NHL season, the hustling Fedorov continued to increase his scoring.

in the regular season. In the 11 playoff games he scored 5 goals and 5 assists. He finished second to Guy Carbonneau in voting for the Selke Trophy, awarded to the league's top defensive forward (and in fact he received more first-place votes than Carbonneau). Nevertheless, some critics placed part of the blame for the Red Wings' playoff disappointment on Fedorov's shoulders.

The team's management saw the matter differently. The front office spent the summer trying to trade Yzerman to bolster the defense, a move that would have allowed Fedorov to take a permanent place as the team's premier forward. But the Wings could not make the deal they wanted. They kept Yzerman and traded for high-scoring Dino Ciccarelli, a right wing who had scored 38 goals and 38 assists for the Washington Capitals.

In the 1992–93 season, Fedorov continued to raise his scoring little by little, posting 34 goals and a total of 87 points. Together, Fedorov, Yzerman, and Ciccarelli gave Detroit the most potent offense in the Campbell Conference. With improved scoring, the Red Wings won 47 games to finish

second in their division. But goalie Tim Cheveldae was overworked in goal, and the team still
could not put together a corps of defensemen good
enough to keep the pressure off him. In the playoffs the team was eliminated in seven games by
the Toronto Maple Leafs, and this spelled the end
of Bryan Murray's reign as coach.

For Fedorov, his third season in the NHL brought
some stability. He took over the center spot on the
Wings' second line, and he joined Yzerman and
Ciccarelli as the team's power-play forwards. The
thrill of celebrity and the excitement of playing in
the NHL were starting to wear off, however. He
was beginning to understand that the numbers
and statistics you put up in the regular season
don't mean much without the one thing that cer-
tifies greatness—the Stanley Cup.

TRIUMPH AND DISAPPOINTMENT

4

The 1993–94 season brought changes both for Fedorov and for the Red Wings.

First, Red Wings owner Mike Ilitch made a move that many observers saw as reflecting his strong commitment to reverse the team's postseason failures and bring Detroit its first Stanley Cup since 1955: he moved coach Bryan Murray up to the front office, naming him general manager, and gave the coaching job to Scotty Bowman. Bowman had been a big winner at his previous coaching stops. He had won the Stanley Cup five times with the Montreal Canadiens and then had guided the Pittsburgh Penguins to the title in 1991–92 and 1992–93.

Bowman arrived with the reputation of an old-time coach who accepted no excuses from his players. He had been dismissed by Pittsburgh after just two seasons when the Penguins tired of his strict discipline. By bringing in Bowman, Ilitch

Fedorov crosses the blue line on his way to scoring a goal against the Calgary Flames in January 1995.

seemed to be challenging his players, saying, "Win the Cup now, or else."

But fate threw a monkey wrench into the plans. On October 21, Yzerman suffered a herniated disk in his neck that would put him out of action for two months. Bowman immediately turned to Fedorov for relief. He put the 23-year-old Russian on the top line with Ciccarelli and Slava Kozlov, another young Russian whom Fedorov was helping adjust to life in the NHL.

The Red Wings lost 7 of their first 10 games, stumbling after the loss of their captain and leading scorer. Then things turned around. Over a 33-game stretch after their initial slump, the Red Wings posted a 22–7–4 record. Fedorov led the charge. With the burden for scoring placed on his shoulders, Fedorov did not wilt, nor did he slow down when Yzerman returned. In the team's first 50 games Fedorov racked up 32 goals and 43 assists.

The league's defensemen took notice, but the pounding they administered had little effect. All season long, Fedorov ran neck and neck with the "Great One," Wayne Gretzky, for the league scoring title. In the end Gretzky took that honor, but Fedorov won just about everything else. He became the first European player to win the Hart Trophy as the league's Most Valuable Player (MVP). He also won the Selke Trophy as the top defensive forward, and he was named the best player in the league by the *Hockey News*, the *Sporting News*, and *Hockey Digest*.

The prize that meant the most to him, though, was the Lester Pearson Award, the MVP award voted by the league's players themselves. This honor meant that the people he skated against night after night recognized that he was the most dangerous man on the ice.

In mid-December 1993 Fedorov puts the puck past New York Rangers goalie Glenn Healy for his 23rd goal of the young season. By the end of the season, Fedorov had 56 goals, 120 points, and a mantel full of awards.

But what had been a brilliant season for Fedorov ended in disaster. Although the Red Wings finished first in the Norris Division, they were embarrassed in the first round of the playoffs by the San Jose Sharks, who beat them in seven games. Owner Mike Ilitch went back to the drawing board. He fired General Manager Bryan Murray, giving Bowman control over personnel. Veteran goaltender Mike Vernon was brought in to teach Chris Osgood, whose rookie mistakes had been blamed for the Wings' early playoff exit. Bowman also went after some tougher role players, who could make opponents pay for trying to beat up on Fedorov, Yzerman, Ciccarelli, or Kozlov.

The team looked like a genuine Stanley Cup contender, but a dispute between the NHL and the players' union put the 1994–95 season on hold. The league had hired former National Basketball Association (NBA) executive Gary Bettman as commissioner, and he brought with him the idea of imposing a limit, or "salary cap," on the amount of money that each team could pay its players. Even though basketball players' salaries had continued to soar under the NBA's cap, the NHL Players Association feared that the same would not be true for hockey players. It was not until January 1995, with the season almost half gone, that the dispute was resolved. The league scrambled to put together an abbreviated season of 48 games.

When the delayed season finally began, it turned out to be less than a stellar year for Fedorov. He suffered his first serious injury, missing six games with a separated shoulder. And after a year in which he could do no wrong, suddenly it seemed he could do no right. His 20 goals and 30 assists did not quiet his critics, who said he was loafing, resting on the laurels he had won the previous season.

Maybe Fedorov provoked criticism because so much of what he did on the ice seemed easy for him. When he broke an opponent down or put a perfect cross-ice pass through a defender's legs, he did it so

Fedorov (center) congratulates Dino Ciccarelli for scoring a goal in the first game of the 1995 Stanley Cup finals against New Jersey. But goals were rare for the Red Wings in this series, and they lost to the brawny Devils in four games.

smoothly, so effortlessly, that it was easy to wonder why he didn't do that every time he touched the puck. His own skill made it easy to forget just how good he was.

For the second year in a row, the Red Wings won their division—now renamed the Central Division. With a stiffened defense, and with Vernon and Osgood sharing the duties at goalie, the Wings marched through the first three rounds of the playoffs with a 12–2 record.

The Stanley Cup finals, though, matched the New Jersey Devils' brawn against the Red Wings' speed, and brawn won, hands down. The Devils had no identifiable star other than goalie Martin Brodeur, but they used a bruising defense to hold the Wings in check, sweeping Detroit in four games.

Bowman called Detroit's performance an embarrassment to the NHL. Vernon had failed to provide the quality goaltending that was expected of him, Bowman could not find an answer to the Devils' fierce trapping defense, and individually no Detroit player—not Yzerman, not Ciccarelli, and not Fedorov—could find a way to take charge.

When the Red Wings walked down the line, shaking the Devils' hands after Game 4, they saw where they wanted to be. They saw the elation in their opponents' eyes, and they realized—maybe for the first time—just how much winning the Stanley Cup means.

A BROKEN WING?

When Nike began making hockey skates in 1995, the giant shoe company naturally looked for a rising young star on a winning team to endorse the new product. A decade before, Nike had made one of the smartest moves in business history when it signed a young guard from the University of North Carolina to put his name on a basketball shoe. The Air Jordan sneaker would reap a fortune for both Michael Jordan and Nike president Phil Knight.

No doubt some old-time hockey purists were shocked when Nike decided to put its white skates on a 24-year-old Russian, but anyone who had watched a Red Wings game had to admit that the commercial that launched Nike's hockey line was not all that farfetched. In the commercial, Fedorov puts on a dazzling display of skating and stick-handling around and through a seemingly endless assault of defensemen. When he finally gets

Chicago Blackhawks goalie Jeff Hackett stops a shot by Fedorov in March 1996.

to the net, he makes a nifty move on the goalie and slips the puck past him. The only thing that can stop Fedorov is the Zamboni, the huge ice-smoothing machine.

Despite the ad's technical merits, Nike's timing was wrong. After the New York Rangers won the Stanley Cup in 1994, the NHL had seemed to be on the verge of matching baseball, football, and

Slava Kozlov (left) and Fedorov were two of the talented "Russian Five" who the Red Wings hoped would lead the team to a Stanley Cup.

basketball in popularity in the United States. Instead, the labor dispute that disrupted the 1994–95 season turned many new fans away, and the lackluster play in the 1995 Stanley Cup finals drove off still more.

If anything could draw fans back, it would be the vision of Fedorov, with the dazzling skills of a figure skater, dancing around one lumbering thug after another. Unfortunately, soon after the ad appeared in January 1996, Fedorov wasn't skating around anybody. That spring he slipped into the worst slump of his career.

He still finished the season with 107 points—his second season above 100. He broke a team record with 11 game-winning goals, and he was second in the league in plus-minus rating (which indicates how well the player's team does when he is on the ice). Moreover, the Red Wings won a team-record 62 games. But Fedorov was criticized for scoring just 39 goals, down from his high of 56 in 1993–94.

Fedorov's performance was all the more disappointing because Detroit had surrounded him with a group of Russian stars that Coach Scotty Bowman hoped would spur him to reach the heights he had achieved in his MVP year of 1993–94. Fedorov played much of the season in a unit that featured forwards Igor Larionov and Slava Kozlov and defensemen Vladimir Konstantinov and Slava Fetisov. By reuniting Fedorov with his former Central Red Army teammates Larionov and Fetisov—the hockey idols of Fedorov's generation in Russia—Bowman wanted to remind him of how great he had been.

But the tactic seemed to have the opposite effect. Although Fedorov used his skills to set up his teammates, he avoided creating shots for himself—and when he had them, he often passed them up.

Then came the playoffs—and another post-season failure for the Red Wings. The team's regular-season success made the playoff woes even harder to understand. For an answer, everyone looked at Fedorov. In the playoffs he racked up a league-leading 18 assists but scored only 2 goals in 19 games. The Red Wings failed to return to the Stanley Cup finals, knocked out in six brutal games by the eventual champions, the Colorado Avalanche.

Red Wings owner Mike Ilitch started looking for offers for Fedorov. Surprisingly, only the arguments of Bowman—the coach who had so often feuded with his young star during the season—kept Fedorov on the team.

Fedorov's problems did not end with the conclusion of the Red Wings' season. He played for Russia in the World Cup games, and when Russia finished without a medal, the press in his homeland blasted Fedorov, saying he had become fat and lazy with his newfound wealth.

When Fedorov returned to the Red Wings in the fall, for the first time he seemed leery of the media and even of the fans. He had heard his critics on both sides of the globe, and he didn't like the sound. There was more than just his reputation at stake. Fedorov was in the last year of his contract. With a big season, he could become one of the highest-paid players in the NHL. But if he couldn't break out of the slump, he might find himself looking for a job.

That year Fedorov had brought his father to Detroit. Viktor Fedorov started training American youngsters in Russian-style hockey, and he also found time to help his son. Sergei said he trained

May 1996: Fedorov, at left, throws his arms around Coach Scotty Bowman as teammates pile on Steve Yzerman. Yzerman's goal advanced the Red Wings to the Western Conference finals, where they lost to the Colorado Avalanche.

harder that summer than he had since joining the NHL. If there were any truth to the accusations of Russian reporters that Fedorov was lazy or out of shape, he would put those doubts to rest. "Do I look fat?" he asked the media. "I remember what I left behind in Russia. The bread lines. The Russian Mafia. I'm still the same man I was in Russia."

At first, though, his hard work seemed to have little effect. When the 1996–97 season began, Fedorov could not buy a goal, and even his passing was off. In Detroit's first 16 games he had a measly three goals and six assists. The shots were there, he said, but he could not find the net. He said he was working harder than ever, but somehow no one seemed to believe him.

Things were so bad that when the NHL sent a film crew to Detroit to film Fedorov for a promotional ad, Bowman reacted in disgust, wondering aloud, "When are they going to catch on?"

Fedorov did the only thing any athlete can do: he kept working. Eventually there were glimpses of the greatness he had once shown. In a game against the Montreal Canadiens, he threaded the gap between a pair of defenders, accelerating just as the two closed in on him. Then he froze the goalie with a fake and put the puck into the net over the goalie's shoulder.

Fedorov had been playing left wing in a unit with Larionov and Kozlov. Now Bowman, noted for getting the most out of players, moved Fedorov to the second line and put him at center, where he was most able to use his unique talents. Like a point guard in basketball, the center runs the offense. He carries the puck up the ice, setting up the wings or—if the opportunity presents itself—taking the puck to the goal himself.

In late December 1996 Fedorov had a brilliant game, scoring all five Red Wings goals in a stunning 5–4 overtime victory over Washington. Detroit trailed 4–2 in the third period before Fedorov scored twice to tie the game. Then, at 2:39 of overtime, he took a pass from Konstantinov and snapped a wrist shot past the Capitals' goalie. Fedorov tried to downplay the achievement, recalling what one of his early coaches had told him: What you've done in a game is already history. In the morning you go out and practice again.

The modesty was appropriate, because in the following games Fedorov again played inconsistently. When placing him at center on the team's second line failed to spark him, Bowman put him on the checking line, and then even made him a defenseman. This meant long minutes on the ice for Fedorov—something he had always wanted—but defense was hardly the position he wanted to play. He ended the regular season with just 30 goals and 33 assists, the poorest statistics of his career. Few people expected him to be a major force in the playoffs. But he was about to prove the doubters wrong.

One thing that eased Fedorov's situation was the fact that the rest of his teammates had been playing very well. Even with Fedorov's slump, the Wings finished second in the Central Division, third overall in the Western Conference. In the first round of the playoffs the Wings faced the St. Louis Blues, a team they felt confident about beating.

Although the Blues had compiled a mediocre record in the regular season, they shocked Detroit in the first game, holding the Red Wings scoreless for a 2–0 victory. Detroit took the next two games, but St. Louis again put the clamp on the Wings in a 4–0 shutout in Game 4. With the series even, Bowman knew he had to shake his team up and find some scoring.

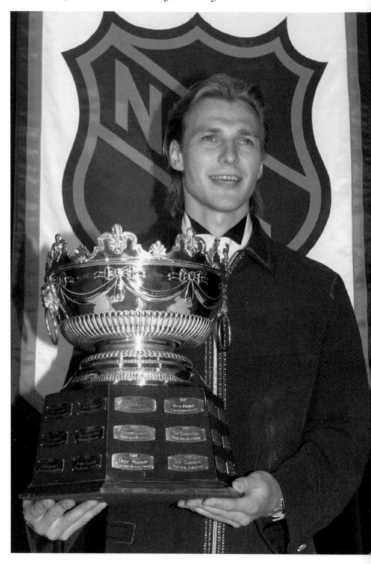

Despite his long slump that began in early 1996, Fedorov won the 1996 Selke Trophy as the NHL's top defensive forward.

The coach decided it was time to reunite the Russian Five—Fedorov, Larionov, Kozlov, Konstantinov, and Fetisov—on the same unit. The reunion immediately proved successful. Fedorov contributed assists in both Game 5 and Game 6 as the Red Wings took the series, making the game look easy.

In the second round the old Fedorov was back. In a four-game sweep of the Anaheim Mighty Ducks, he scored a pair of goals—including the game-winner in Game 3—and three assists. Three times he helped set up his linemate Slava Kozlov for goals.

That left the Colorado Avalanche as the last roadblock in the Wings' path to the finals. The relationship between the two teams was not good. In the 1996 playoffs, the Avalanche had given the Wings a thorough beating not only on the scoreboard but on the ice. During the regular season the bad feelings had grown whenever the two teams met. Fights erupted on the ice, and taunts were exchanged in the media.

With this background, experts thought the 1997 playoff series would be won by the team that hit the hardest. Instead, the victory went to the team that skated the fastest. After losing the first game in Denver, the Red Wings took control of the series with three straight victories, including a 6–0 pounding of the Avalanche in Game 4. The Russians, and Fedorov in particular, played excellent hockey.

In Game 6, on the verge of elimination, the Avalanche targeted Fedorov for abuse, repeatedly crushing him into the boards throughout the first period. Finally the pounding took its toll. After one especially vicious hit, Fedorov had to be helped to the locker room. He could scarcely breathe, and

Knocked out of the game by a vicious hit, Fedorov shows his heart by coming back to score the winning goal in Game 6 against the Colorado Avalanche, May 26, 1997.

doctors feared he might have a couple of broken ribs.

When the first period ended, team captain Steve Yzerman came to Fedorov in the locker room and told him his teammates needed him on the ice. Do whatever you need to, Yzerman begged, but get back in the game.

Fedorov came back, and he scored the game-winning goal—his third goal of the series—in the Red Wings' 3–1 victory, lifting his team into the Stanley Cup finals for the second time in three years. This performance answered once and for all any questions about Fedorov's toughness and heart. Along with his 3 goals in the series, Fedorov had contributed 4 assists. The Russians as a unit had scored 9 of Detroit's 16 goals. Bowman looked like a genius for his reunion of the Russian Five, and Fedorov was a player reborn.

In the finals the Wings faced the Philadelphia Flyers, the same kind of physical team as the New Jersey Devils, who had swept them out of the play-offs in 1995. The Flyers featured the Legion of Doom, a huge and talented line anchored by the hulking Eric Lindros, but they were no match for Detroit's Legion of Vroom.

Fedorov put away Game 1 midway through the second period when he and Yzerman skated in against Flyers goalie Ron Hextall. The Wings' captain flipped the puck back to Fedorov in the right circle, and Fedorov beat Hextall with a slapshot, giving Detroit a 3–1 lead in the eventual 4–2 victory.

In Game 2 the Red Wings prevailed by the same score on the Flyers' home ice. Now they started to dream about sweeping the series.

The Flyers scored the first goal of Game 3 to take their first lead of the series, but that seemed only to fuel the Wings' drive. Yzerman quickly tied the game by slipping the puck through Hextall's legs. Less than two minutes later, Fedorov put Detroit ahead to stay when he scooped the puck away from the Flyers' Karl Dykhuis, dashed toward the waiting Hextall, and beat him with a wrist shot from between the circles. Fedorov later scored again on a power play as the Red Wings posted a 6–1 victory.

After such a dominating performance, it seemed that the only team that could keep Detroit from a sweep was the Red Wings themselves. They refused to slack off, fighting to a 2–1 victory in Game 4. At last this talented team had won the Stanley Cup.

For Fedorov the win was twice as sweet because his contribution had been so great. After the worst season of his career, he had come back to play the best hockey of his life when his teammates needed him the most.

But the celebration was short-lived. Six days after the Red Wings won the Cup, a limousine was carrying Vladimir Konstantinov, Slava Fetisov, and the team's massage therapist, Sergei Mnat-sakanov, back from a team golf outing. When the limo crashed, Fetisov and the driver escaped with minor injuries, but Konstantinov and Mnatsakanov were both left in comas, clinging to life.

Later, Fedorov said that his Stanley Cup cele-bration ended the night of the crash. The next night, many of the team's fans held a vigil at the scene of the accident, and Fedorov joined them. He quietly thanked the fans and asked them to pray for his friends' recovery. It was a side of Fedorov—the easygoing young man who was so flashy on the ice—that most had not seen before.

This was not the self-centered egotist that the

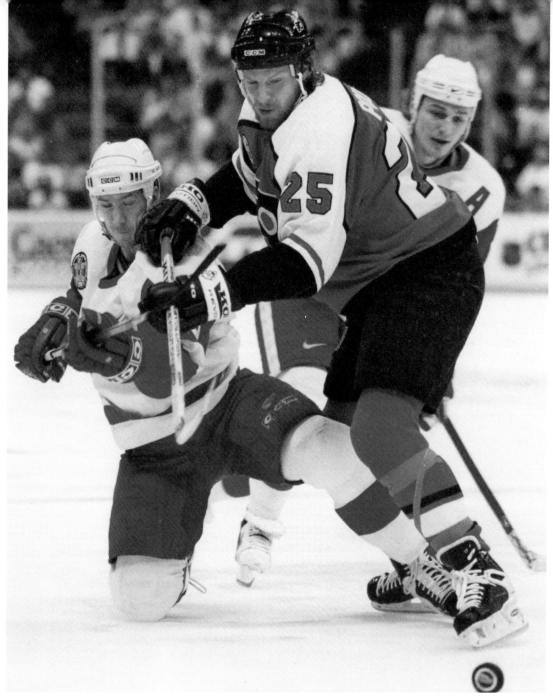

*Shjon Podein of the Flyers knocks the Red Wings'
Slava Kozlov off the puck in Game 3 of the 1997
Stanley Cup finals, with Fedorov trying to reach in
from behind. As the Flyers discovered, muscle was
not enough to beat the Wings.*

press and some of his teammates would later try
to make him seem during his contract holdout.
Fedorov was a man so stricken by the misfortune
of his friends that the greatest triumph of his own
career held no sweetness for him. For the Red
Wings' supporters who saw him that night, it was
a rare glimpse into the heart of a hero.

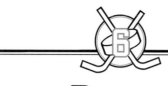

BACK IN
THE GAME

When he returned to the Red Wings in February 1998 after his five-month holdout, Fedorov made peace with his teammates off-ice the way a rookie would. On their first road trip, he invited the whole team out to dinner—at his expense. Of course, if he had been a rookie, they might have shown a little restraint in their dinner orders. Considering Fedorov's huge new contract, however, the Red Wings chose lobster, filet mignon, and the finest champagne. Fedorov was happy to oblige.

The promise he had made to Ilitch—that he would earn every penny—would have been meaningless to his teammates. For them, he had to regain their respect in other ways. Most important, he would have to prove his value on the ice.

Fedorov may not have been in mid-season rhythm like his teammates, but there was not a great deal of rust on him. In one game soon after his return, facing Wayne Gretzky and the New

Fedorov talks to the press after Game 3 of the 1998 Stanley Cup finals—a game in which he scored a very special goal.

York Rangers at Madison Square Garden, Fedorov won an astounding 21 of 24 faceoffs. Overall, for the 21 regular-season games he played, his numbers were respectable though not spectacular: 6 goals, 11 assists, 2 game-winning goals. There was little criticism of his play.

To a large extent, the Red Wings had become a team on which stars didn't matter. Sure, they had Yzerman, Brendan Shanahan, Larionov, Fedorov, Nicklas Lidstrom, and the rapidly improving Slava Kozlov—but the teamwork made individual accomplishments secondary. In fact, the biggest fear about Fedorov's return was not that he would not perform, but that he might perform too well—that he would feel the need to be the star every night to prove he was worth the money he was being paid. If so, even if he racked up big numbers, he might disrupt the chemistry on a team that was chasing its second straight Stanley Cup.

It turned out that Fedorov fit in better than anyone could have hoped. His speed and his stickhandling once again made him the center of attention every time he took a shift on the ice, but this served to take the pressure off his teammates. He didn't have to score. And like the rest of the Wings, he didn't pay much attention to his own statistics. He focused on how many games the team won.

Again the Red Wings cruised into the playoffs. In the first two rounds, as Detroit beat the Phoenix Coyotes and St. Louis Blues, Fedorov scored a league-best eight goals and added seven assists. Cynics may have said Fedorov was looking for the $12-million payday he would get if the Red Wings made the conference finals. But if he was just playing for the money, he certainly earned it.

In Game 4 of the St. Louis series, when Detroit

needed a victory on the Blues' ice to take a lead of three games to one, Fedorov assisted on Slava Kozlov's goal 72 seconds into the third period. This put Detroit ahead, 3–2. Then Fedorov scored with the Red Wings shorthanded to stretch the lead to two goals. He capped the night with an empty-net goal in the closing moments.

The Dallas Stars, the Red Wings' opponent in the conference finals, realized that Fedorov was having an impact. The Stars assigned bruising defenseman Derian Hatcher the task of knocking Fedorov off his game. For five games Hatcher did keep him from scoring either a goal or an assist. "I took a couple of hard punches in the face," Fedorov admitted. "It was bad because I took them pretty well—like a boxer, pretty hard."

Nevertheless, the Red Wings' depth and balance once again carried them to victory. In each game a different player stepped up, and in the final game Fedorov found the net again, scoring a goal less than two minutes into the second period that gave Detroit a 2–0 lead and seemed to break the Stars' spirit.

The Wings entered the Stanley Cup finals as overwhelming favorites over the Washington Capitals. In the first game of the series, however, it was hard to tell why. A heat wave was afflicting the city of Detroit, and there were problems with the ice inside Joe Louis Arena. Fedorov suggested there were even bigger problems with the Wings themselves. "We got a lead and then we stood out there chewing gum or something," he said afterward, adding that maybe they were too happy just to be back in the finals. Despite their sluggishness, the Red Wings managed a 2–1 victory.

In Game 2 the Caps took a two-goal lead, and Slava Kozlov, who was leading the team in points, went to the locker room with an injury. Late in the game, the Red Wings finally began playing in earnest. When Yzerman scored shorthanded seven minutes into the third period, he ignited a three-goal rally. Doug Brown tied the game, despite playing with a broken nose, and Kris Draper scored the game-winner in overtime.

Although Fedorov did not have a goal or an assist in that game, Coach Bowman gave him much of the credit for the victory. Fedorov had peppered Washington goalie Olaf Kolzig with a phenomenal 13 shots in the game. In the coach's mind, the workout he gave the Caps' star goalie was worth more than an assist or two.

Game 3 was scheduled for the anniversary of the crash that had left Konstantinov with serious brain injuries. To a man, the Red Wings said they would have preferred not to play on that date. The day before the game, as the team was in the locker room preparing to leave for the airport, Fedorov approached Konstantinov's old locker, which had been kept unused. While the other Wings joked and packed their bags, Fedorov made a quiet promise to his friend: "Next game, Vladdie, it will be one year. I'll get a goal for you."

The next night, the Wings outplayed the Capitals on both ends of the ice. Because of Kolzig, however, Washington managed to stay in the game. When Brian Bellows scored for the Caps with just over nine minutes left, the game was tied, 1–1.

Fedorov had yet to keep his promise. The Caps had learned from the way the Stars had played Detroit. They kept a big forward on Yzerman and used defenseman Calle Johansson to pound Fedorov. But this strategy couldn't work forever.

With just under five minutes left, Doug Brown had the puck near center ice when he saw Fedorov

Washington's Olaf Kolzig stops a shot by Fedorov in Game 2 of the 1998 Stanley Cup finals. In that game Fedorov barraged the goalie with 13 shots.

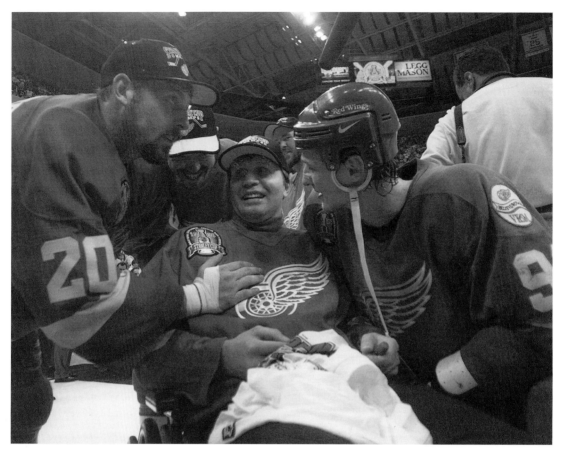

Fedorov (right) and Martin LaPointe (left) celebrate the Red Wings' 1998 Stanley Cup win with former teammate Vladimir Konstantinov, who had been injured in a limousine crash the year before.

alone on the right side. He pushed a pass ahead to Fedorov, who accelerated along the boards. Johansson came to meet the speedy Russian as he started to cut toward the goal. Fedorov changed direction, moving toward the middle of the ice and the slot. As Johansson tried to follow him, Fedorov fired a wrist shot through the defenseman's legs that Kolzig did not see coming until it was too late.

That move won the game. It was a move only Fedorov could make.

It may have been the crucial goal of the series. The Red Wings completed their Stanley Cup sweep with a 4–1 victory in Game 4, a game in which the Capitals seemed to have already surrendered.

With that final goal—his 10th of the 1998 play-offs—Fedorov helped lift his team to its second straight Stanley Cup championship. He also reminded any remaining skeptics why he was worth the money the Red Wings were paying him. And most important, he made good on the promise to his friend.

STATISTICS

Season	Team	Regular Season					Playoffs				
		GP	G	A	PTS	PIM	GP	G	A	PTS	PIM
1990–91	Det	77	31	48	79	66	7	1	5	6	4
1991–92	Det	80	32	54	86	72	11	5	5	10	8
1992–93	Det	73	34	53	87	72	7	3	6	9	23
1993–94	Det	82	56	64	120	34	7	1	7	8	6
1994–95	Det	42	20	30	50	24	17	7	17	24	6
1995–96	Det	78	39	68	107	48	19	2	18	20	10
1996–97	Det	74	30	33	63	30	20	8	12	20	12
1997–98	Det	21	6	11	17	25	22	10	10	20	12
Totals		527	248	361	609	371	110	37	80	117	81

GP   games played
G   goals scored
A   assists
PTS   points (goals plus assists)
PIM   penalties in minutes

Chronology

1969	Sergei Fedorov is born on December 13 in Pskov, Russia (then part of the Soviet Union).
1978	Moves with his family to Apatiti, a small town above the Arctic Circle near Finland.
1985	Leaves his family to go to Moscow and play for the Soviet Central Red Army team.
1988	Scores 6 goals and records 6 assists in just 6 games to lead the Soviet Union to the silver medal at the World Junior Championships.
1989	Leads the Soviet Union to the gold medal at the World Championships. On the trip back to the Soviet Union, his teammate Aleksandr Mogilny defects to join the National Hockey League. In the NHL Entry Draft that year, the Detroit Red Wings choose Fedorov, thus obtaining the right to sign him if he leaves the Soviet Union. During the winter, he tours the NHL with the Central Red Army team, playing in Canada and the United States.
1990	Again plays on the gold-medal-winning Soviet team at the World Championships. In July he leaves the Soviet team in Portland, Oregon, as it is preparing for the Goodwill Games and goes to Detroit to join the Red Wings, setting off a war of words between the NHL and the Soviet Hockey Federation. In the end, the Red Wings pay the Soviets a signing fee to resolve the controversy.
1990–91	Finishes second to goaltender Ed Belfour for Rookie of the Year after totaling 31 goals and 48 assists in 77 games.
1991–92	Selected for the NHL All-Star Game for the first time. Finishes as runner-up to Guy Carbonneau for the Selke Trophy, given to the league's best defensive forward, even though he receives more first-place votes than Carbonneau.
1992–93	Improves point production for the third straight year, finishing with 34 goals and 53 assists.
1993–94	With team captain Steve Yzerman injured, Fedorov steps into leadership role. Scores 56 goals and adds 64 assists for 120 points. Becomes the first European-born player to win the league MVP award, the Hart Trophy. Also wins the Selke Trophy and the Lester Pearson Award, given to the best player in the league as chosen by the other players.

1994–95   Leads the league in playoff points (24) and assists (17), but the Red Wings lose the Stanley Cup finals to New Jersey.

1995–96   Sets a franchise record for the most game-winning goals in a season with 11. His plus-minus rating of +49 is second best in the league.

1996–97   Scores 5 goals in a 5–4 overtime victory over Washington in December. Despite being criticized for much of the season, he leads the team in the playoffs with 8 goals and 12 assists as the Red Wings win the Stanley Cup. Vladimir Konstantinov, his best friend on the team, is severely injured in a limousine accident shortly afterward.

1997–98   Begins the season with a contract holdout. In January, the Russian Olympic hockey team makes him a last-minute addition, and he helps Russia win the silver medal, leading the team in total points and minutes played. With a new contract, Fedorov rejoins the Red Wings in late February and becomes the leading goal scorer in the playoffs as Detroit wins another Stanley Cup.

FURTHER READING

Bynum, Mike, editor. *Quest for the Cup.* Detroit: The Detroit News/Triumph Books, 1997.

Fishler, Stan. *Fishler's Illustrated History of Hockey.* Toronto: Warwick, 1993.

Klein, Jeff, and Karl-Eric Reif. *The Coolest Guys on Ice.* Atlanta: Turner, 1996.

Larionov, Igor, with Jim Taylor and Leonid Reizer. *Larionov.* Winnipeg: Codner, 1990.

Murphy, Austin. "A Red Hot Wing." *Sports Illustrated,* January 24, 1994.

Schoenfeld, Bruce. "Star Search." *The Sporting News,* April 17, 1995.

Wigge, Larry. "Wings of a Dynasty." *The Sporting News,* June 22, 1998.

Wigge, Larry. "A World of Difference." *The Sporting News,* February 21, 1994.

ABOUT THE AUTHOR

Dean Schabner has worked for United Press International for nearly a decade as both a sports writer and a news reporter. He covers the NHL and the NBA as well as the summer and winter Olympics. He has won a Pushcart Prize for his short fiction. He lives in New York City.

INDEX

Anaheim Mighty Ducks, 44
Bandy, 13–14
Belfour, Ed, 25
Bellows, Brian, 54
Bettman, Gary, 34
Bowman, Scotty, 31, 33, 35, 39, 40, 41, 42, 43, 46, 54
Brodeur, Martin, 35
Brown, Doug, 54, 55–56
Buffalo Sabres, 20
Bure, Pavel, 17, 18
Burr, Shawn, 24
Calder Trophy, 25
Carbonneau, Guy, 28
Carolina Hurricanes, 9
Carson, Jimmy, 26
Central Red Army team, 8, 14, 17, 18, 39
Cheveldae, Tim, 29
Chicago Blackhawks, 27
Ciccarelli, Dino, 28, 29, 32, 33, 34, 35
Colorado Avalanche, 40, 44–46
Dallas Stars, 53
Detroit Red Wings
    and Fedorov's defection, 13–14, 20–21, 23–24
    limousine accident, 8, 47
    major personnel changes, 28, 31, 33, 39
    owner, see Ilitch, Mike
    winning Stanley Cup, 7, 8, 47, 56–57
Draper, Kris, 54
Dykhuis, Karl, 47
Fedorov, Sergei
    childhood and youth, 16–18
    contract disputes, 8, 9–10, 51
    criticized, 28, 34, 39, 40, 41
    defection from Soviet Union, 8, 13–14, 20–21
    as defenseman, 26–27, 43
    early days in NHL, 25–26
    and fans, 7, 8, 10–11, 26, 27, 40, 47, 49

honors, 25, 32, 43
injuries, 34, 44–46
in international competitions, 9, 18, 40
reaction to Konstantinov's injury, 8–9, 47–49, 54, 57
in slump, 39–43
style of play, 7–8, 24–25, 26–27, 34–35, 52
television commercial featuring, 37–39
troubles with Red Wings teammates, 9, 10, 51
Fedorov, Viktor Alexandrovich, 16, 40
Fetisov, Slava, 9, 18, 39, 44, 47
Florida Panthers, 7
Goodwill Games, 13, 20–21
Gretzky, Wayne, 32, 51
Hart Trophy, 32
Hatcher, Derian, 53
Healy, Glenn, 33
Hextall, Ron, 46, 47
Ilitch, Mike, 10, 13, 25, 31–32, 33, 40, 51
Johansson, Calle, 55, 56
Jordan, Michael, 37
Kasatonov, Aleksei, 18
Klima, Petr, 25
Kolzig, Olaf, 54, 55, 56
Konstantinov, Vladimir, 39, 42, 44, 56
    injury in limousine accident, 8, 47, 54
Kozlov, Slava, 32, 33, 38, 39, 42, 44, 52, 53–54
Land training, 15
LaPointe, Martin, 56
Larionov, Igor, 9, 11, 18, 19, 39, 42, 44, 52
Legion of Doom (Philadelphia Flyers line), 46
Lidstrom, Nicklas, 11, 52
Lindros, Eric, 46
Makarov, Sergei, 17
Miller, Kelly, 26

Mnatsakanov, Sergei, 47
Mogilny, Aleksandr (Alexander), 17, 18
    defection to NHL, 19–20
Montreal Canadiens, 31, 42
Murray, Bryan, 26, 29, 31, 33
New Jersey Devils, 34, 35, 46
New York Rangers, 38, 51–53
Nike shoe commercials, 37–39
Olympic Games, 9, 16
Osgood, Chris, 33, 35
Pearson Award, 32
Philadelphia Flyers, 46–47
Phoenix Coyotes, 52
Pittsburgh Penguins, 31
Priakin, Sergei, 19
Russia
    evolution of ice hockey in, 14–16
    as source of players for NHL, 19
    training in, 15
    See also Soviet Hockey Federation
"Russian Five," of Detroit Red Wings, 38, 39, 44, 46
Salary cap, and 1994–95 NHL labor dispute, 34
San Jose Sharks, 33
Selke Trophy, 28, 32, 43
Shanahan, Brendan, 17, 52
Shank, Daniel, 24
Soviet Hockey Federation, 19, 23
Soviet Union. See Russia
St. Louis Blues, 26, 43, 52–53
Tikhonov, Viktor, 18
Toronto Maple Leafs, 29
Vernon, Mike, 33, 35
Washington Capitals, 28, 42, 53–57
Yashin, Alexei, 18
Yzerman, Steve, 26, 28, 29, 32, 33, 35, 41, 46, 47, 52, 54, 55
    role in recruiting Fedorov, 18–19